THOMAS CRANE PUBLIC LIBRARY

QUINCY MASS

CITY APPROPRIATION

CONNECTING THE 21ST CENTURY TO THE PAST:
What Makes America America? (2000-the present)

HOW AMERICA BECAME AMERICA

TITLE LIST

THE NORTHERN COLONIES: FREEDOM TO WORSHIP (1600-1770)

THE SOUTHERN COLONIES: THE SEARCH FOR WEALTH (1600-1770)

AMERICA IS BORN (1770-1800)

THOMAS JEFFERSON AND THE GROWING UNITED STATES (1800-1811)

WARS AT HOME: AMERICA FORMS AN IDENTITY (1812-1820)

REMEMBER THE ALAMO: AMERICANS FIGHT FOR TEXAS (1820-1845)

AMERICANS MOVE WEST (1846-1860)

THE CIVIL WAR: AMERICA TORN APART (1860-1865)

AMERICAN WILDERNESS: ALASKA AND THE NATIONAL PARKS (1865-1890)

BEYOND OUR SHORES: AMERICA EXTENDS ITS REACH (1890-1899)

A SHIFTING ROLE: AMERICA AND THE WORLD (1900-1912)

AMERICA IN THE 20TH CENTURY (1913-1999)

CONNECTING THE 21ST CENTURY TO THE PAST: WHAT MAKES AMERICA AMERICA? (2000-THE PRESENT)

HOW AMERICA BECAME AMERICA

CONNECTING THE 21ST CENTURY TO THE PAST:
What Makes America America? (2000-the present)

BY MICHELLE QUINBY

MASON CREST

CONNECTING THE 21ST CENTURY TO THE PAST

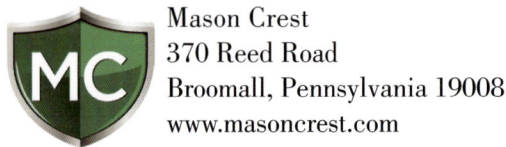

Mason Crest
370 Reed Road
Broomall, Pennsylvania 19008
www.masoncrest.com

Copyright © 2013 by Mason Crest, an imprint of National Highlights, Inc. All rights reserved. No part of this publication may be reproduced or transmitted in any form or by any means, electronic or mechanical, including photocopying, recording, taping, or any information storage and retrieval system, without permission from the publisher.

Printed and bound in Hashemite Kingdom of Jordan.

First printing
9 8 7 6 5 4 3 2 1

Library of Congress Cataloging-in-Publication Data

Quinby, Michelle.
 Connecting the 21st century to the past : what makes America America, 2000-the present / by Michelle Quinby.
    p. cm. — (How America became America)
  ISBN 978-1-4222-2409-0 (hardcover) — ISBN 978-1-4222-2396-3 (series hardcover) — ISBN 978-1-4222-9319-5 (ebook)
 1. United States—Politics and government—Juvenile literature. 2. United States—Economic conditions—Juvenile literature. I. Title.
  JK40.Q85 2013
  973—dc23

                              2012010416

Produced by Harding House Publishing Services, Inc.
www.hardinghousepages.com
Cover design by Torque Advertising + Design.

CONTENTS

Time Line 6

1. The Declaration of Independence 9

2. The Constitution 17

3. The Electoral College 27

4. Civil Rights 35

5. What Makes the American Economy? 41

Find Out More 46

Index 47

About the Author and the Consultant 48

CONNECTING THE 21ST CENTURY TO THE PAST

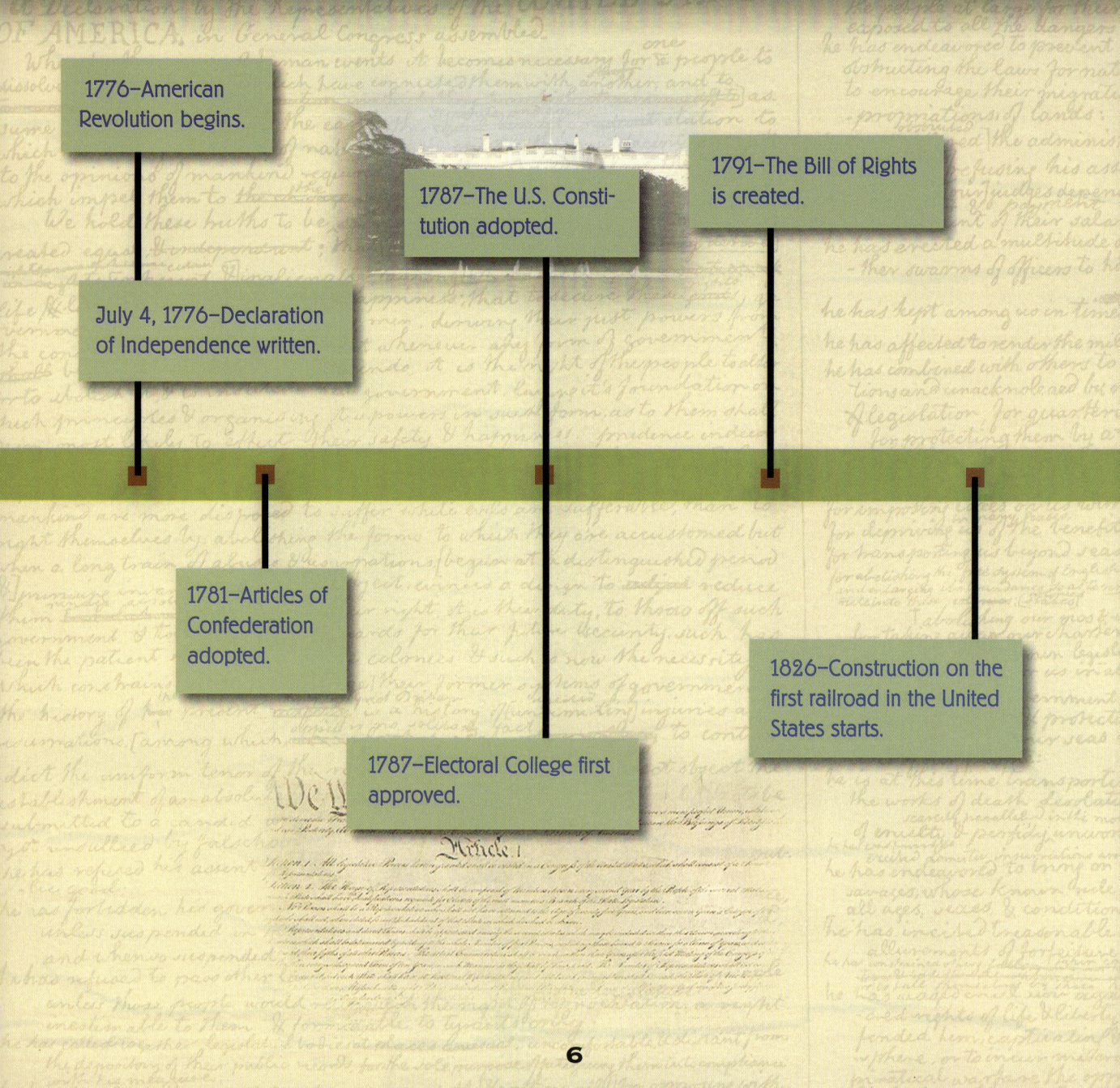

- 1776–American Revolution begins.
- July 4, 1776–Declaration of Independence written.
- 1781–Articles of Confederation adopted.
- 1787–The U.S. Constitution adopted.
- 1787–Electoral College first approved.
- 1791–The Bill of Rights is created.
- 1826–Construction on the first railroad in the United States starts.

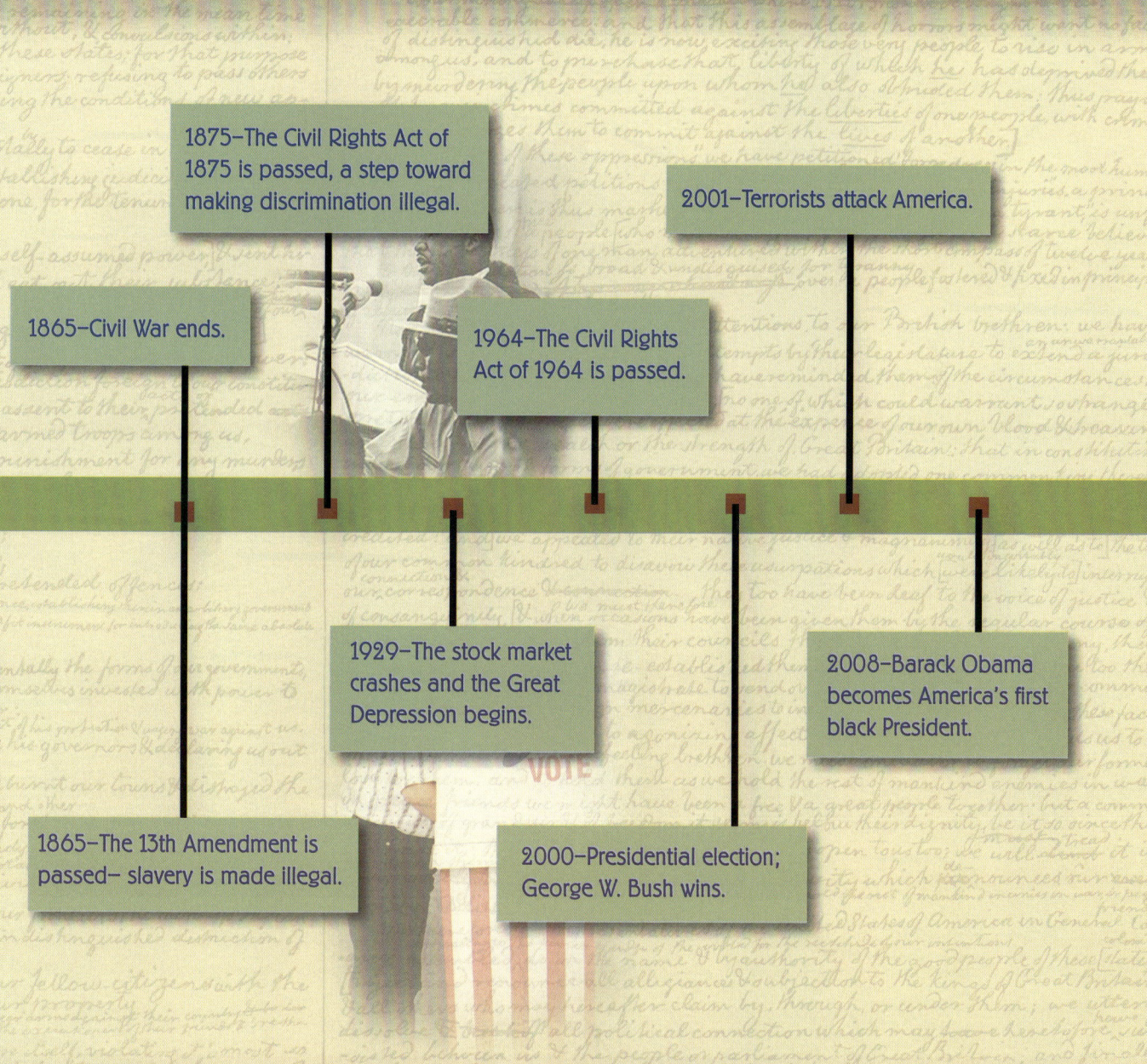

"It is to secure our rights that we resort to government at all."
—Thomas Jefferson

Chapter One
THE DECLARATION OF INDEPENDENCE

Over the past 250 years, a lot has changed in America. The United States has grown bigger. Modern inventions, wars, and twenty-first century ideas have changed the way we think.

But some things haven't changed. At the center of the United States are very important ideas. They shaped the country when it was born. And they continue to shape it today.

You can find many of these ideas in the documents that people wrote when the United States was very young. The Declaration of Independence is one of them.

WHAT IS THE DECLARATION OF INDEPENDENCE?

A long time ago, the United States used to be thirteen different **colonies**. These colonies were run by Great Britain. They didn't have their own government.

Many people were unhappy with Great Britain. They didn't like how it was running the colonies.

Colonies are groups of people living in a different land but still belonging to their home country.

CONNECTING THE 21ST CENTURY TO THE PAST

At first, people just wanted to fix the relationship between Great Britain and the colonies. They didn't want the colonies to actually become their own country.

But then things changed. In 1776, colonists and British soldiers fought a couple of battles at Lexington and Concord in Massachusetts.

During this time, a group of men were meeting together. They called themselves the Continental Congress. There were people from each colony in the group. Together, they talked about what to do.

Pretty soon people realized that the colonies would have to declare independence. They would form their own country.

The Congress asked Thomas Jefferson to prepare a formal argument for **independence**. The group of men would send it to Great Britain. They would also read it to the colonists. It would be called the **Declaration** of Independence.

Thomas Jefferson

IDEAS

Thomas Jefferson represented Virginia in the Continental Congress. He was young

---

Independence is another word for freedom—the ability to make decisions without anyone telling you what to do.

A **declaration** is a statement of something.

THE DECLARATION OF INDEPENDENCE

DECLARATION OF INDEPENDENCE FAST FACTS

Who wrote the Declaration?
    Thomas Jefferson

When was it signed?
    July 4, 1776

Where was it written?
    Philadelphia, Pennsylvania

Who signed it?
    Men from all thirteen American colonies.

Why was it written?
    To explain to the world why the colonists needed to separate from Great Britain.

CONNECTING THE 21ST CENTURY TO THE PAST

The original Declaration of Independence has faded with age.

and smart. The other representatives knew he was a good writer.

Jefferson actually wrote the Declaration of Independence. But he didn't just pull the ideas he wrote about out of his own head. He got them from other great thinkers.

Americans wanted their new country to be a **democracy**. They didn't want a king. The Declaration of Independence declared that the new country would practice democracy.

Jefferson also used ideas from a man named John Locke. Locke believed that all people had certain right.s He said that people had the right to health, freedom, and life, just because they are human. Americans today still think those things are very important.

Another important idea that Jefferson used was that the government couldn't be too powerful. It couldn't hurt people just because it wanted to. It had to be fair. That wasn't how things had always worked with Great Britain.

Democracy is a form of government where people choose their own leaders by voting.

12

THE DECLARATION OF INDEPENDENCE

WRITING

Jefferson and a few other men set to work. They came up with the Declaration of Independence. It had four parts.

The first part is called the preamble. It talked about the reasons the colonists were writing the Declaration.

The second part talked about the rights each human being should be guaranteed.

The third part was a long list of reasons why colonists were unhappy with the British king. This part was trying to prove that the king didn't deserve to rule the colonists.

The last part was the actual declaration. It said that the colonies would fight to be free from Great Britain.

Here's a short quote from the Declaration of Independence:

*"We hold these truths to be **self-evident**, that all men are created equal; that they are endowed by their Creator with certain **inalienable** rights; that among these are life, liberty, and the pursuit of happiness."*

Something that is **self-evident** is obvious. It doesn't need to be proven, because you can tell it's true just by looking at it.

Something that is **inalienable** can't be taken away. It's a part of what makes something what it is.

CONNECTING THE 21ST CENTURY TO THE PAST

WHAT ABOUT WOMEN?

Unfortunately, when the United States was born, women were considered to be not exactly human in the same way that men were. This meant that they didn't have the same rights that men did. In fact, they could be treated much like property that belonged to men. Women's rights would come later to America. Smart, brave women looked at the ideas that shaped America—and insisted that those ideas belonged to women as much as men.

WHAT HAPPENED NEXT

Now the colonists had declared that they wanted to be independent from Great Britain. Next they fought the Revolutionary War. And they won. The United States was born. The Declaration of Independence—the document that had started it all—would continue to be important to Americans.

The importance of the Declaration of Independence changed over time, though. Not too many people paid attention to it right after the war against Britain was won. There were more important things to worry about. They did celebrate July 4, though—the day the Declaration of Independence was signed.

During the Civil War in the 1860s, Abraham Lincoln made the Declaration important again. He talked about it in his famous speech called the Gettysburg Address. Lincoln was

The Declaration of Independence

arguing that the United States was founded on a new idea: that all humans are created equal and that all people have rights. It was his argument to end slavery.

These ideas are still very important to the United States. The country doesn't always live up to them—but the fact that they are there, right at the center of the U.S. government's birth, means that they're wonderful goals for Americans to always move toward.

EQUALITY IN TWENTY-FIRST-CENTURY AMERICA

One of the big issues in twenty-first-century America is whether people who are the same sex have the right to marry. Some people say no, they shouldn't have this right. These people believe that marriage should only be between a man and a woman. Many people believe this is a religious issue. Other people, however, say that homosexuals are facing discrimination when their right to marry is denied.

What do you think? Do you believe that homosexuals' right to marry is protected by the U.S. Constitution's guarantee of human rights? Or do you think that states should have the power to deny homosexuals the right to marry?

Chapter Two
THE CONSTITUTION

The most important document in the United States is the Constitution. It tells us what our government should look like. It tells us what is legal and illegal. It's at the heart of the United States.

THE BEGINNING

After the United States was born—after the colonists had won the Revolutionary War against Great Britain—it was time to set up a government.

First, the leaders of the new nation came up with the Articles of **Confederation**. That was a document that created America's first government. The central **federal** government was pretty weak, though. Americans wanted to make sure there wouldn't be a king in the United States. Instead, the state governments had a lot more power than the government at the center had.

Many people didn't like this first government. They wanted to start over. In 1786, Congress agreed to call people together to replace the Articles of Confederation.

A **confederation** is a group of countries or states working together.

Federal has to do with the government that controls an entire country.

CONNECTING THE 21ST CENTURY TO THE PAST

The next year, men from every state met together again. They decided to come up with a new document. They would call it the United States Constitution.

GUIDING IDEAS

The main problem that the men faced was that they needed to create a strong government that could protect the country. But it couldn't be too strong. Who would control the government?

The men decided they would make the federal government stronger. Then it could control the state governments. Each level—the nation and the states—would have different powers. Neither would get too strong.

The government would have three branches. There would be an **executive** branch. That was the President and his staff. There would be a judiciary branch. That's the court system and judges. And there would be the legislative branch. That would be Congress, who made and passed laws.

Each branch would have its own power. Nobody would have too much power though. They kept an eye on each other. It was a system of checks and balances designed to keep any single branch of the government becoming too strong.

The country would be ruled by the majority. That means that more than half of the people had to agree on something. Then it could become part of the government.

At the same time, the government had to protect the rights of the **minority**. The people who didn't agree with everyone else couldn't end up in jail because they spoke out. They couldn't be hurt.

An **executive** is someone who has power to run things.

A **minority** is a smaller group of people that is different in some way from the rest of the people in the larger group to which they belong.

The Constitution

CONNECTING THE 21ST CENTURY TO THE PAST

Capitol Building, Washington, D. C.

The Constitution

The United States government would also be a democracy. People would vote. They would pick other people to represent them in the government. Then those people would make the laws and run the country.

ARGUMENTS

Of course, it was hard for everybody to agree. Arguments broke out. The Constitution ended up being a **compromise** in a lot of ways.

Some states had a lot of people and some states didn't. The smaller ones were afraid that their voice wouldn't be heard in government. Everyone would listen to the bigger states. They wanted all states to have the same number of votes in the government.

Bigger states didn't like that plan. They had more people! It was only fair that they have more votes, they said. The small states would be too powerful for their size.

The men came up with a solution. The U.S. Congress would have two different groups of representatives.

The Senate was made up of two representatives from each state. That made the small states happy.

The House of Representatives would be based on population. Each state would have a different number of representatives according to how many people lived there. That made the bigger states happy.

Another compromise was about slavery. Some people from the North didn't like slavery. Many people from the South didn't want to give up slavery. However, no one was ready to fight about whether or not slavery was right. That would have to wait.

A **compromise** is when each side of an argument gives in a little bit and finds a way to meet in the middle.

CONNECTING THE 21ST CENTURY TO THE PAST

For now, they had to figure if slaves would count as people. To us, we think that's a silly question. Of course slaves were people! They were human beings who were treated cruelly. But back then, slaves weren't considered members of the government. They couldn't vote. They didn't get the same protections as free people.

The Southern states had a lot of slaves. If the slaves counted in the population, those states would have a lot more representatives. The Northern states didn't want to count them. It wasn't fair to the states without slaves, the North said.

In the end, everyone agreed to count each slave as three-fifths of a person. The Southern states could get more representatives. But not too many more. This seems like a really stupid compromise today, since clearly slaves were not pieces of persons—but since they couldn't vote, they had no say in the government. By allowing them to be counted at all, the South would get more power in the government.

CHANGING THE CONSTITUTION

The Constitution was really short. It didn't cover everything that could ever happen with the government. But the creators of the Constitution made sure that people could change it and add to it as time passed.

The government can amend the Constitution. That means it can be changed and added to. It's hard to do though. The Constitution has twenty-seven amendments today. An amendment has to be really important to become part of the Constitution. Some of the more important amendments have:

- provided for the direct election of senators
- freed slaves

- given women the vote
- lowered the voting age to eighteen

THE BILL OF RIGHTS

The Bill of Rights is part of the Constitution. It's actually just the first ten amendments. In other words, it is the first ten things that people added to the Constitution.

Sometimes we take the Bill of Rights for granted. Of course all people have the right to say whatever they want! Of course people can't be put in jail without a trial! But if we didn't have the Bill of Rights, the government could take our freedom away. It could not let people say what they wanted. It could put whomever it wanted in jail.

Here are some of the things that the Bill of Rights gives us:

- the right to practice any religion we want
- the freedom of speech
- the right to meet together
- the right to a fair trial
- the right to carry weapons
- protection from torture

TACKING ON THE BILL

At first, the Constitution didn't include a Bill of Rights. Then, once it was written, the Bill of Rights was only meant to limit the power of the national government. No one wanted it taking over people's lives. Later, the Bill of Rights applied to state governments too.

CONNECTING THE 21ST CENTURY TO THE PAST

People still argue about what the Bill of Rights means. The Supreme Court makes the decision about whether something a government does goes against the Bill of Rights. But each judge on the Supreme Court has slightly different ideas.

The Constitution and the Bill of Rights are still very important today. It shapes everything the government does. We still believe that the things the Constitution says are the best ways to run the country.

TWENTY-FIRST-CENTURY AMERICA AND STATES' RIGHTS

Some of the issues that Americans argued about back in the 1700s are still being argued about today. For example, Americans don't always agree on how much power states should have compared to the nation's central government. Some Americans believe that the individual states should have the right to decide about big issues like same-sex marriages, protecting the environment, and abortion. Other Americans think that the central government should pass laws that will apply to the entire United States regarding these issues, so that everyone in America will be governed by the same laws.

KEEPING AMERICANS SAFE IN THE TWENTY-FIRST-CENTURY

On September 11, 2001, America was attacked by terrorists. The terrorists were people who wanted to change the way America treated Muslim nations by making Americans afraid. The terrorists flew planes into buildings in New York City and Washington, D.C. Thousands of people were killed.

Suddenly, Americans were scared. No enemy had attacked America's homeland for nearly 200 years. Americans wanted their country to make them safe again. They wanted a strong central government to protect them. In response to this, a new government agency was formed, called the Department of Homeland Security.

Without the strong central government that started to take shape when America was born, the United States could not have formed this powerful protection agency. The states would have had to fight terrorism on their own.

Vote Here

Chapter Three
THE ELECTORAL COLLEGE

You might think that we choose the president by voting for him (or her!). Each person gets one vote, as long as he or she is at least eighteen. That's true. But it's a little more complicated.

In 2000, the United States had a presidential election. George W. Bush ran against former Vice President Al Gore. Gore won half a million more individual votes than Bush. But Bush won 277 votes in something called the Electoral College. Gore only won 266. Because Bush had more Electoral College votes, he became President.

The Electoral College is obviously pretty important. After all, it decides who the President is going to be.

Back when the Constitution was created, the writers didn't think a whole lot about picking the President. Everyone knew that George Washington would be the first President. After that, they thought that Congress would be involved in picking the Presidents.

A little later, people started thinking about it more. They came up the idea of the Electoral College.

CONNECTING THE 21ST CENTURY TO THE PAST

HOW THE ELECTORAL COLLEGE WORKS

The **founders** of our country didn't think people could pick a President all by themselves. They didn't believe anyone would unite behind just one or two people. They didn't have easy ways of communication back then either. There were no phones or computers. It would be hard for everyone to talk to each other and pick a President.

The Electoral College was the solution. It would be made up of representatives from each state. The number of representatives depended on how many members of Congress each state has.

The representatives wait for each state to vote. One **candidate** will win the most votes in that state. Then the representatives all vote for whoever won in their state. A couple states do it a little differently, but that's how it usually happens.

Whichever candidate gets the most Electoral College votes then becomes President.

PROBLEMS

The College worked all right for a while. Then the election of 1800 caused some problems.

At the time, each Electoral College representative could vote twice. The person with the most votes became President. The person with the second-most votes became the Vice President.

In 1800, Thomas Jefferson and man named Aaron Burr tied. They had the same number of votes!

Founders are people who build the beginnings of something.

A **candidate** is someone who is running for office or who is asking to be chosen for some position.

THE ELECTORAL COLLEGE

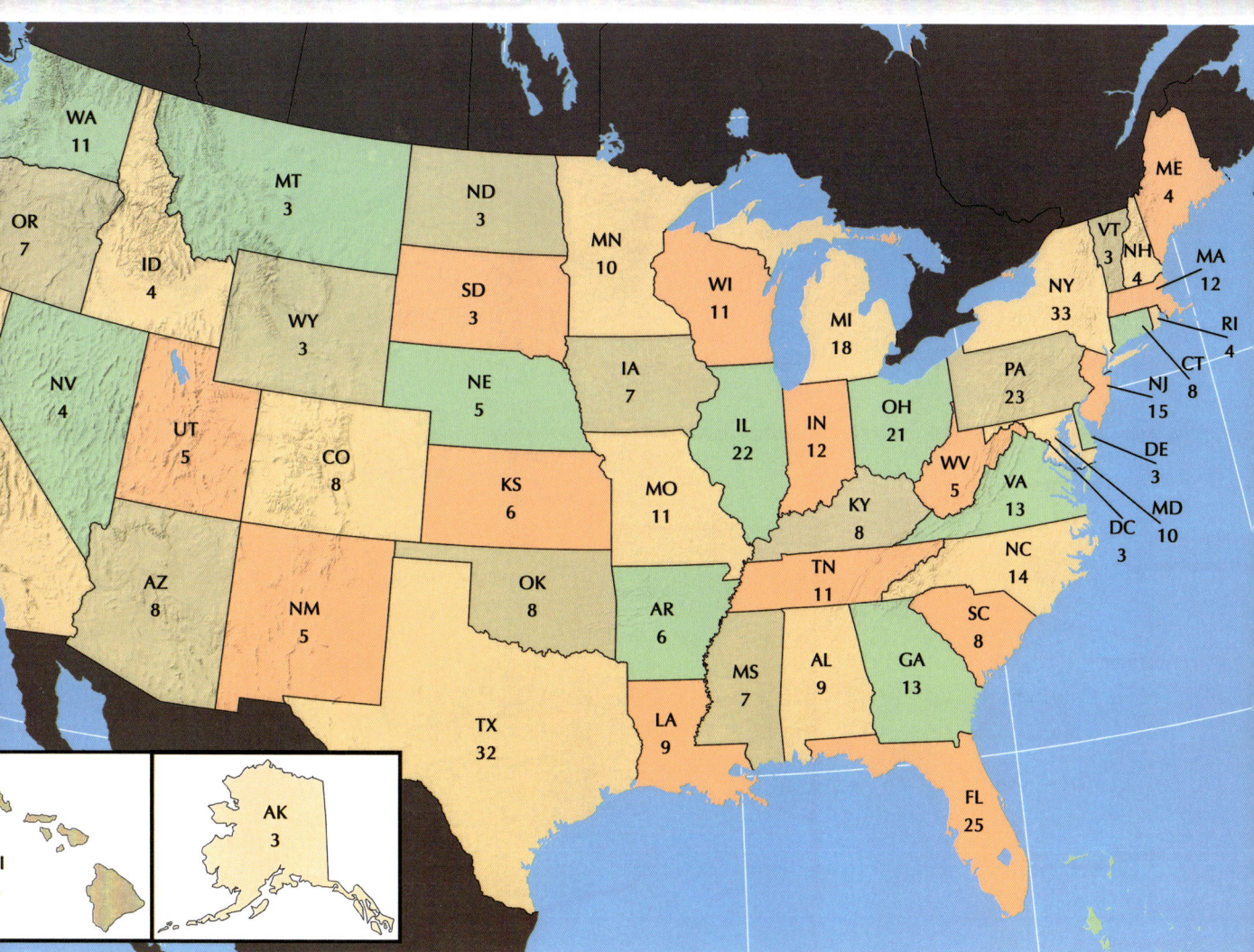

Electoral map showing the number of votes each state has in the Electoral College

CONNECTING THE 21ST CENTURY TO THE PAST

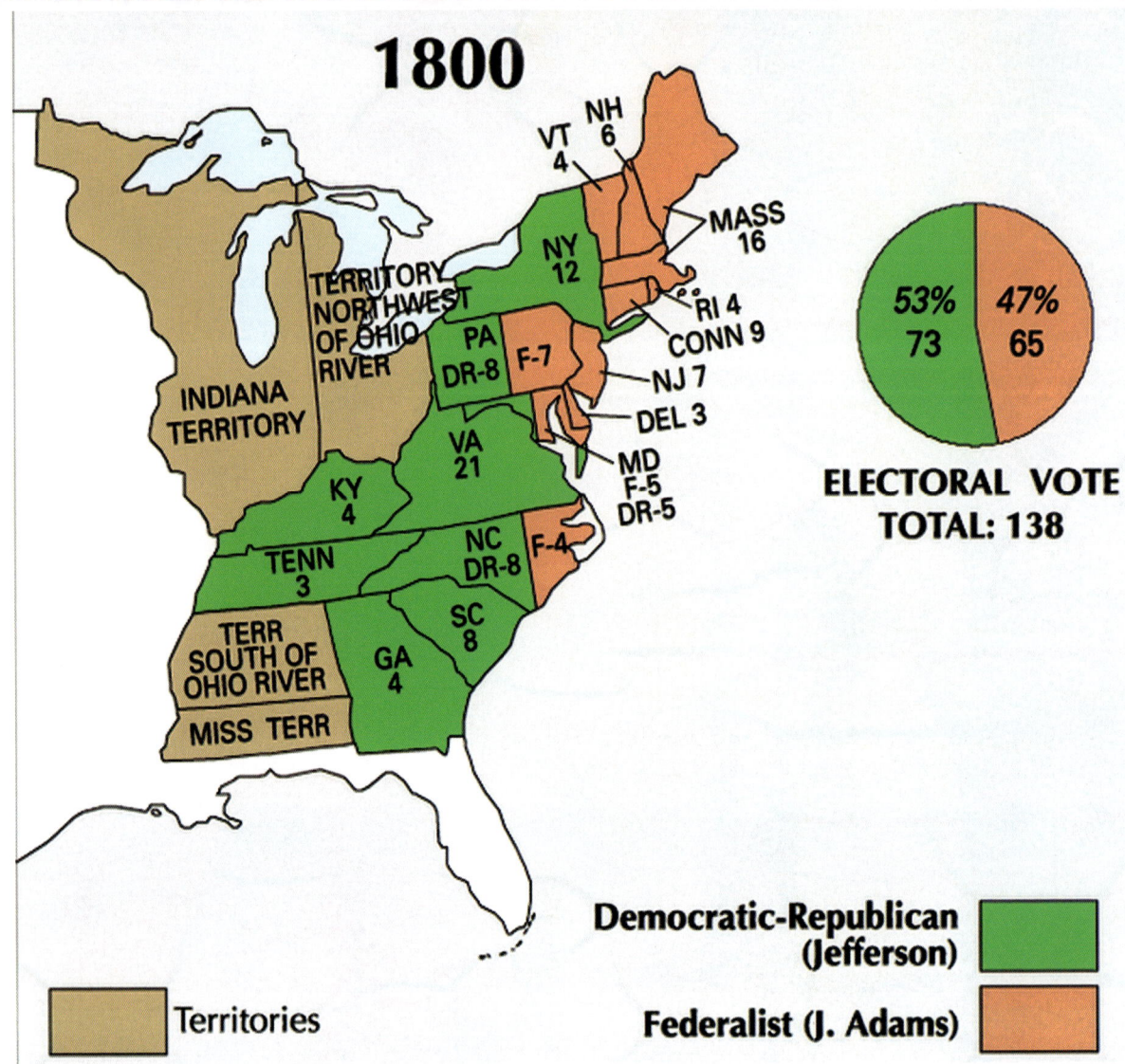

Map of presidential election, 1800

THE ELECTORAL COLLEGE

The House of Representatives eventually chose Jefferson. But it was a tough choice. It made a lot of people angry.

So the government added another amendment to the Constitution. Electors had to cast one vote for President and one vote for Vice President. The winner has to get at least 270 votes.

TWO PARTIES

Today there are two main political groups of people in the United States: the Republicans and the Democrats. They are our political parties.

The reason that we only have two parties is partly because of the Electoral College. Because you have to get so many votes in the College, you have to have lots of support. Convincing a lot of individual people to vote for you is hard. It's easier to convince one political party.

The symbols of America's political parties: Democratic donkey and Republican elephant

THE ELECTORAL COLLEGE IN THE TWENTY-FIRST CENTURY

Many Americans were upset by the 2000 election, where Al Gore, the Democratic candidate, had 543,895 more individual votes than George Bush, the Republican candidate—and yet Bush became the President, based on the Electoral College's vote. In the end, the Supreme Court got involved as well, making a decision not to recount votes. The country moved on—but this was the beginning of a major split in the country between Republicans and Democrats. Bad feelings between the two parties grew. Many Democrats felt that Al Gore should have been the President.

Today, some people think America needs a new way to elect its Presidents. They say that the Electoral College doesn't work in the modern world—and that it's not fair that more people can vote for someone to be President and yet that person can still end up not being the President.

What do you think?

The Electoral College

Capitol Hill Building, Washington D. C.

A candidate has to be strong enough to win most of the votes in a state. Then he or she gets the Electoral College votes for that state. People from third parties find it really hard to get the most votes. So they never win a whole state and its Electoral College votes.

There aren't too many third party people who ever have a chance of being the President. There are alternatives to the Democrats and the Republicans. But they're never popular enough to really have a say in the government.

Chapter Four
CIVIL RIGHTS

The spring of 1963 was hard in Birmingham, Alabama. Martin Luther King Jr. and his followers were fighting for rights for all African-Americans. They were doing it without violence. They **protested** peacefully.

But the police did use violence. They used attack dogs and tear gas. It was more than a hundred years after the Civil War, but for a while, it seemed like the war was still being fought.

The Civil Rights Movement, as this time in America's history is known, did a lot to change America. It helped African Americans and others gain some rights. But the struggle wasn't over.

To really understand why the color of a person's skin mattered in 1963—and why it still matters today—we have to go back in history.

THE CONSTITUTION

When the Constitution was written, slavery was legal. A lot of people had slaves. All slaves were African Americans. Their ancestors had been brought here in the 1600s and the 1700s.

The Civil War was fought in part to end slavery. The South wanted to hang on to the practice of slavery. Southerners needed slaves to grow crops on their farms. They didn't

Protested means that someone stood up and spoke out against something that's unfair.

CONNECTING THE 21ST CENTURY TO THE PAST

think of slaves as human beings who were equal to white people. Many Northerners didn't like slavery. The North didn't really have slavery by the time the Civil War broke out.

The North won the Civil War, and slavery was banned. The Thirteenth Amendment to the Constitution ended slavery.

The next amendment said that all people born in the United States were citizens. Before that, African Americans weren't citizens.

Finally, the Fifteenth Amendment made sure that all citizens could vote (but not women). Any man could vote, no matter what his race or color was.

Not everybody followed this rule. Whites tried to keep blacks from voting in many states. For example, some states made people pay money when they voted. Blacks couldn't usually afford to pay it. This meant that the only people who ended up voting were whites.

Later on, the government got rid of these practices. It made more laws that made sure that all people could vote.

Civil rights demonstrator

LATER LAWS

For a long time, blacks weren't treated the same as other Americans. They weren't slaves any more, but there was still a lot of **racism** around.

In 1875, Congress passed the Civil Rights Act of 1875. It made it illegal for anyone to

CIVIL RIGHTS

refuse to serve someone because of his or her race. It was the first law that made **discrimination** illegal.

Unfortunately, it didn't really apply to individual people who didn't work for the government. The United States would make more laws later, though.

In 1896, the Supreme Court decided that "separate but equal" was okay. Black people and white people could be separated in train cars or buses or stores. That is called segregation. But the things for black people had to be just as good as the things for white people. The court case was called *Plessy versus Ferguson*. Today we think that is racist and wrong.

More laws eventually ended segregation. The Civil Rights Movement in the 1960s made people listen. The government eventually passed a lot of laws.

The Civil Rights Act of 1964 is the most important. It ended a lot of discrimination against African Americans. No public places could separate blacks and whites any more.

Today, race is still an issue. We haven't solved it yet. Black people (and others, like Latinos), don't always get the same treatment as white people. It's a fight we'll keep on fighting.

Lyndon Johnson signing the Civil Rights Act

Racism is when people treat others differently—and unfairly—because of the color of their skin.

Discrimination is unfair treatment of a group of people based on the color of their skin, their religion, their sex, or some other thing that sets them apart.

CONNECTING THE 21ST CENTURY TO THE PAST

DISCRIMINATION IN TWENTY-FIRST-CENTURY AMERICA

One of the big issues in modern America is immigration. Should the United States let people easily cross its borders from Mexico and other countries? Some people say yes—other people say no, America should keep Mexicans and others from entering the United States so easily. Some Americans also believe that those who are here illegally—without the government's permission—should be sent back to where they came from. But other Americans believe that this is a form of discrimination against Latinos.

Latinos are a group of people who come from Latin America. Latin America includes Central America, South America, and the Caribbean. Most Latinos speak Spanish. They come from a lot of different countries, though. People from Mexico are Latino. People from Puerto Rico are Latino. People from Chile are Latino. Some Latinos are immigrants. They just moved to the United States recently. They were born in another country.

CIVIL RIGHTS

Other Latinos were born in the United States. Their families have been here for a long time.

Latinos are the fastest growing group of people in the United States today. Latino culture is changing the United States. We now eat Latino food, like tacos and nachos. We sing along to Latino musicians. Some of us are even learning Spanish. But some Americans worry that Latinos will change America so that it is no longer the country that was created in 1776. Other Americans, however, insist that the United States has always been a nation of immigrants—and that people from around the world help to make America stronger.

What do you think?

Barack Obama was America's first black President.

Chapter Five
WHAT MAKES THE AMERICAN ECONOMY?

The economy is a word that has to do with all the ways that a country produces money. It has to do with businesses and farms, jobs and stores. The economy is the big picture that includes all these things.

People from other countries often think about money when they think about America. They watch TV shows and movies that show rich Americans. So they think all Americans are rich.

Many Americans have a lot more money than people have in other parts of the world. They can afford food, homes, and cars. They don't have to worry about money.

Many other Americans don't actually have much money. Their jobs don't pay them enough. Or they can't find a job. People from other countries don't always understand that.

You need a lot of money to live in this country. Houses, cars, cell phones, and other things are expensive!

But overall, the United States is a pretty rich country. People don't usually starve to death. Many people do have jobs that let them live comfortably. Why is it that the United States has so much money?

WAY BACK

Part of the answer has to do with the Revolutionary War. One reason the colonists didn't like the British was because of how the British dealt with money.

CONNECTING THE 21ST CENTURY TO THE PAST

Many colonists had their own businesses. They believed that the money they made was for them. They didn't want to give it away.

The British thought a little differently. They liked people who had their own businesses. But the point of a business, the British thought, was to make the whole government strong. It wasn't just for individual people to make money.

The colonists thought the British government was too involved in their businesses. The British ended up taking a lot of money from the colonists through taxes. The colonists wanted it for themselves.

Then the colonists won. They made sure the government wasn't like Britain. They protected businesses from the government.

It mostly worked really well. People made a lot of money. People's lives got better.

KEEPING UP

Later on, more things helped Americans make money. People could trade things across state lines. That helped everyone become richer. Unlimited trade doesn't always work so well, but it did in the United States.

Copyright laws were important. These meant that anyone who invented something could claim it as theirs. Then they were free to sell their idea. Or they could use it to make money.

Communication around the country got better. A postal system was set up. A person in Florida could send a letter to a person in Maine. That made doing business with other people a lot easier.

In the 1800s, railroads became a big deal too. Trains crossed the whole country. People could now easily ship something they were selling to people who wanted to buy it in another part of the country.

All these things helped American businesses get bigger and bigger. And some people got richer and richer.

What Makes the American Economy?

BIG BUSINESS

Sometimes businesses got too much money, though. A small business would become successful. Then it grew and grew. It eventually got too much power. It didn't let other businesses succeed.

Railroads were one kind of business that grew to be huge. The railroads gave thousands of people jobs. They made a lot of money. Railroad businessmen had a lot of power in the government. They could make sure that laws that helped them were passed. They could destroy laws that would hurt them.

Huge companies were called monopolies. They were the only ones who could sell things in their business. So if a company had a monopoly selling steel, no other company could sell steel. The big company could make people buy steel for a lot of money. There was nowhere else to buy it.

Some people got richer. But not everyone. The people who ran the businesses got more and more money. They were called "robber barons."

Meanwhile, the people who worked for them did not get richer. They sometimes didn't get much money at all. They had to work in dangerous conditions.

Eventually the U.S. government stepped in. Those businesses were just too big. The government made them smaller. It outlawed monopolies. Smaller businesses could succeed again.

AMERICA TODAY

Most of us take the way we think about money for granted. But Americans have a special understanding of money. The way we spend it, save it, and give it to other people is very American. Other people think about money differently.

CONNECTING THE 21ST CENTURY TO THE PAST

THE AMERICAN ECONOMY IN THE TWENTY-FIRST CENTURY

In 2008, the United States' economy ran into big trouble. Businesses failed. People lost their jobs. The problem just got worse and worse. In the midst of this, President Barack Obama was elected President. He was the first black President America had ever had. Many people were excited that this young, intelligent black man would be leading the country. They placed a lot of hope on President Obama.

President Obama had many ideas about how to fix America's problems. Obama favored a strong central government that would help poor people with health care. He wanted to take action to protect the environment. He wanted to regulate business and place higher taxes on richer Americans. Not everyone agreed with his ideas. Some Americans felt that Obama's plans would take away the freedoms and rights guaranteed to Americans. They felt President Obama was trying to change important things about the way the United States is run. Other Americans agreed with Obama's plans.

What Makes the American Economy?

Some of them wanted him to take even stronger action. In a nation that was still sharply divided between Democrats and Republicans, President Obama had to struggle to find compromises.

These are big questions. Discussions about questions like these have been going on for years and years in the United States. In fact, Americans' right to figure out these answers for themselves is part of what makes the United States so strong!

Some of the time, it works out well. Sometimes it doesn't. The United States has a lot of money problems. But one thing is true. America is America partly because of how we deal with money.

The ideas that shaped the United States come from more than two hundred years ago—but over time, those ideas have been changed by what's gone on in the world. Some ideas still work well for America. Other ideas have needed to be tinkered with a little, so that they work better in the modern world. Sometimes Americans still need to work hard to find ways to live up to the big ideas that formed their nation.

But the important thing is that the United States is built on good ideas—and those ideas still shape what makes America the nation it is today.

FIND OUT MORE

In Books

Burgan, Michael. *The Electoral College.* Mankato, Minn.: Coughlan Publishing, 2007.

Kamma, Anne and Pamela Johnson. *If You Lived When There Was Slavery in America.* New York: Scholastic, 2004.

Landau, Elaine. *The Declaration of Independence.* Danbury, Conn.: Children's Press, 2008.

Taylor-Butler, Christine. *The Constitution of the United States.* Danbury, Conn.: Children's Press, 2008.

On the Internet

The Constitution
www.archives.gov/exhibits/charters/constitution.html

The Declaration of Independence
www.archives.gov/exhibits/charters/declaration.html

The Economy
www.scholastic.com/browse/collection.jsp?id=455

Slavery
www.socialstudiesforkids.com/subjects/slavery.htm

INDEX

Articles of Confederation 17

Bill of Rights 23, 24
Burr, Aaron 28
Bush, George W. 27, 32

Civil Rights Movement 35, 37
Civil War 14, 35, 36
colonies 9–11, 13
Constitution 17–25, 27, 31, 35, 36
Continental Congress 10

Declaration of Independence 9–15
democracy 12, 21
Democrat 31–33, 45

Electoral College 27–33

Gettysburg Address 14
Gore, Al 27, 32

Jefferson, Thomas 9–13, 28, 31

Lincoln, Abraham 14
Locke, John 12

Obama, Barack 40, 44, 45

racism 36, 37
Republican 31–33, 45
Revolutionary War 14, 17, 41

ABOUT THE AUTHOR AND THE CONSULTANT

Michelle Quinby has enjoyed writing ever since she was a little girl. She loves to tell stories that help people understand the world.

Dr. Jack N. Rakove is a professor of history and American studies at Stanford University, where he is director of American studies. The winner of the 1997 Pulitzer Prize in history, Dr. Rakove is the author of *The Unfinished Election of 2000, Constitutional Culture and Democratic Rule*, and *James Madison and the Creation of the American Republic*. He is also the president of the Society for the History of the Early American Republic.

PICTURE CREDITS
Department of the Interior: p. 30
Dover: p. 16, 19
Jose Gil | Dreamstime.com: p. 40
Kamigami | Dreamstime.com: p. 31
LBJ Library photo by O. J. Rapp: p. 37
Library of Congress: p. 6 (bottom), 8, 12, 13
National Archives and Records Administration: p. 1, 7 (top), 34, 36
PhotoDisc: p. 6 (top), 7 (bottom), 26

Photos.com: p. 20
Songquan Deng | Dreamstime.com: p. 33
Studio1: p. 29
Wildside: p. 10

To the best knowledge of the publisher, all other images are in the public domain. If any image has been inadvertently uncredited, please notify Harding House Publishing Services, Vestal, New York 13850, so that rectification can be made for future printings.